Musical Fairy Houses Coloring

We appreciate you selecting our book, buying our coloring book, and helping our tiny business.

We wish you joy when coloring! We thank all of the contributors to this book for their generosity.

On our Amazon website, kindly post a review and some of your lovely colored photos.

www.ingramcontent.com/pod-product-compliance
Lightning Source LLC
Chambersburg PA
CBHW080959290526
45795CB00009B/3001